MUSINGS OF A CHINESE MYSTIC

LIONEL GILES

Kalamos Literary Services LLP
Email: info@kalamos.co.in | editorial@kalamos.co.in

Published in 2026

by

Kalamos Literary Services

ISBN - 978-93-7349-226-1

Introduction

Although Chinese history can show no authentic contemporary record prior to the Chou dynasty, some eleven hundred years before Christ, there is no doubt that a high pitch of civilisation was attained at a much earlier period. Thus Lao Tzŭ was in no sense the first humanising instructor of a semi-barbaric race. On the contrary, his was a reactionary influence, for the cry he raised was directed against the multiplication of laws and restrictions, the growth of luxury, and the other evils which attend rapid material progress. That his lifetime should have coincided with a remarkable extension of the very principles he combated with such energy is one of the ironies of fate. Before he was in his grave another great man had arisen who laid unexampled stress on the minute regulation of ceremonies and ritual, and succeeded in investing the rules of outward conduct with an importance they had never hitherto possessed.

If Lao Tzŭ then had revolted against the growing artificiality of life in his day, a return to nature must have seemed doubly imperative to his disciple Chuang Tzŭ who flourished more than a couple of centuries later, when the bugbear of civilisation had steadily advanced. With chagrin he saw that Lao Tzŭ's teaching had never obtained any firm hold on the masses, still less on the rulers of China, whereas the star of Confucius was unmistakably in the ascendant. Within his own recollection the propagation of Confucian ethics had received a powerful impetus from Mencius, the second of China's orthodox sages. Now Chuang Tzŭ was imbued to the core with the principles of pure Taoism, as handed down by Lao He might more fitly be dubbed "the Tao-saturated man" than Spinoza "the God-intoxicated." Tao in its various phases pervaded his inmost being and was reflected in all his thought. He was therefore eminently qualified to revive his Master's ringing protest against the materialistic tendencies of the time.

Chuang Tzŭ's worldly position was not high. We learn from Ssŭ-ma Ch'ien that he held a petty official post in a small provincial town. But his literary and philosophical talent must soon have brought him into repute, for we find him in frequent contact with the leading scholars of the age, against whom he is said to have defended his tenets with success. It does not appear, however, that he gained promotion in the public service, which is doubtless to be attributed to his own lack of ambition and shrinking from an active career, as we have his personal account of a deputation which vainly tried to induce him to accept the post of Prime Minister in the Ch'u State. Official routine must have proved in the highest degree distasteful to this finely tempered poetic spirit, as it has to many a chafing genius since. Bold in fancy yet retiring by disposition, prone to melancholy yet full of eager enthusiasm, a natural sceptic yet inspired with boundless belief in his doctrine, he was a man full of contradictions, but none the less fitted to make a breach in the cast-iron traditions of Confucianism, if not to draw others after him in the same track. Of his mental development there remains no record. His convictions, as they stand revealed in his great philosophical work, are already mature, if somewhat lacking in consistency; he comes before the public as a keen adherent of the school of Lao Tzŭ giving eloquent and impassioned utterance to the ideas which had germinated in the brain of his Master. Chuang indeed, supplies the prime deficiency of Lao Tzŭ; he has the gift of language which enables him to clothe in rich apparel the great thoughts that had hitherto found their only expression in bare disconnected sayings. These scraps of concise wisdom, which are gathered together in the patchwork treatise known as the *Tao Tê Ching*, seem to have formed the kernel of his doctrine, and he proceeded to develop them in a hundred different directions. It would be unjust, however, to infer from this that there is nothing in Chuang Tzŭ which cannot be traced back to the older sage, or that he was incapable of original thought of distinct and independent value. On the contrary, his mental grasp of elusive metaphysical problems was hardly if at all inferior to that of Lao Tzŭ himself, and certainly never equalled by any subsequent Chinese thinker. His writings also have that stimulating suggestiveness which stamps the product of all great minds. After reading and re-reading Chuang one feels there are latent depths still unplumbed. Moreover, he gives free rein to his own particular fancies and predilections. There are sides of Lao teaching at which he hardly glances, or which he passes over entirely, while in other directions he allows his brilliant imagination to carry him far out of sight of his fountain-head. If the analogy be not too heavily pressed, we may say that he was to the Founder of Taoism what St. Paul was to the Founder of Christianity.

As with Lao Tao forms the centre and pivot of Chuang Tzŭ's whole system; and this imparts real unity to his work, which in other respects appears undeniably straggling and illcompacted. But Tao as conceived by Chuang Tzŭ is not quite the same thing as the Tao of which Lao Tzŭ spoke with such wondering awe. The difference will be better understood after a brief sketch of the gradual development in the meaning of the word. The first meaning of Tao is "road" or "way,"-and in very early times it was used by a figure of speech for the "way" or method of doing a thing. Thus it came to denote a rule of right conduct, moral action, or the principle underlying it. There also grew up in common speech a natural antithesis between the Way of Heaven (T'ien Tao) and the Way of man, the former expression signifying the highest standard of wisdom and moral excellence, as opposed to the blind groping after truth here below. Finally the "T'ien" was dropped, and Tao then stood alone for the great unseen principle of Good dominating and permeating the Universe. The transition is visible in Lao Tzŭ, who was probably the first to employ the term in its transcendental sense, but who also retains the older expression T'ien Tao. In one of his sayings T'ien Tao is practically equivalent to Tao the First

Cause, and must therefore be translated not the Way but the Tao of Heaven. This brings us to the next stage, of which Chuang Tzŭ is the representative. In his writings Tao never seems to mean "way." But he introduces a new element of perplexity by speaking of T'ien and Tao as though they were two co-existent yet perfectly distinct cosmic principles. He also uses the combination T'ien Tao, and it is here that the clue to the difficulty must be sought. The Tao of Heaven is evidently an attribute rather than a thing in itself, and it is T'ien which has now become the First Cause. It is a less impersonal conception, however, than Lao Tzŭ's transcendental Tao, and in fact closely approximates to our own term "God."[1] What, then, is Chuang Tzŭ's Tao? Though by no means always clear and consistent on the subject, he seems to regard it as the "Virtue" or manifestation of the divine First Principle. It is what he somewhere calls "the happiness of God,"—which to the Taoist of course means a state of profound and passionless tranquillity, a "sacred everlasting calm." Now Lao Tzŭ speaks of Tao as having existed before Heaven and Earth: "Heaven," he says, "takes its law from Tao; but the law of Tao is its own spontaneity." With him, therefore, Tao is the antecedent of T'ien, being what modern philosophers term the Unconditioned or the Absolute. As to his T'ien, the ambiguity which lurks therein makes it doubtful whether he had any definite conception of it at all. He simply appears to have accepted the already existing Chinese cosmogony, oblivious or careless of its incompatibility with his own novel conception of Tao. Chuang Tzŭ to some extent removes this ambiguity by reverting to the older usage. He deposes Tao from its premier position as the Absolute, and puts T'ien in its place. Tao becomes a mystic moral principle not unlike Lao Tzŭ's Tê, or "Virtue," and the latter term when used at all has lost most of its technical significance. Thus broadly stated, some such explanation will prove helpful to the reader, though he may still be baffled by a passage like the following: "A man looks upon God[2] as upon his father, and loves Him in like measure. Shall he, then, not love that which is greater than God? " The truth is that neither consistency of thought nor exact terminology can be looked for in Chinese philosophy as a whole, and least of all, perhaps, in such an abstract system as that of early Taoism .

Leaving this somewhat barren discussion as to the relative position of Tao and T'ien, we now come to what was undoubtedly Chuang greatest achievement in the region of pure thought. As in so many other cases, the germ is provided by Lao Tzŭ who has the saying "The recognition of beauty as such implies the idea of ugliness, and the recognition of good implies the idea of evil." Following up this hint, Chuang Tzŭ is led to insist on the ultimate relativity of all human perceptions. Even space and time are relative. Sense-knowledge is gained by looking at things from only one point of view, and is therefore utterly illusory and untrustworthy. Hence, it appears that the most fundamental distinctions of our thought are unreal and crumble away when exposed to the "light of Nature." Contraries no longer stand in sharp antagonism, but are in some sense actually identical with each other, because there is a real and all-embracing Unity behind them. There is nothing which is not objective, nothing which is not subjective; which is as much as to say, that subjective is also objective, and objective also subjective. When he pauses here to ask whether it be possible to say that subjective and objective really exist at all, he seems to be touching the fringe of scepticism pure and simple. But the point is not pressed; he is an idealist at heart, and will not seriously question the existence of a permanent Reality underlying the flow of phenomena. True wisdom then consists in withdrawing from one's own individual standpoint and entering into "subjective relation with all things." He who can achieve this will "reject all distinctions of this and that," because he is able to descry an ultimate Unity in which they are merged, a mysterious One which "blends, transcends them all."

Still keeping Lao Tzŭ in sight, our author draws further curious inferences from this doctrine of relativity. Virtue implies vice, and therefore will indirectly be productive of it. In any case, to aim at being virtuous is only an ignorant and one-sided way of regarding the principles of the universe. Rather let us transcend the artificial distinctions of right and wrong, and take Tao itself as our model, keeping our minds in a state of perfect balance, absolutely passive and quiescent, making no effort in any direction. The ideal then is something which is neither good nor bad, pleasure nor pain, wisdom nor folly; it simply consists in following nature, or taking the line of least resistance. The attainment of this state, and the spiritual blessings accruing therefrom, constitute the main theme of Chuang Tzŭ's discourse. His whole duty of man is thus summed up and put into a nutshell; "Resolve your mental energy into abstraction, your physical energy into inaction. Allow yourself to fall in with the natural order of phenomena, without admitting the element of self."

This elimination of self is in truth the substitution of the ampler atmosphere of Tao for one's own narrow individuality. But Tao is not only inert and unchanging, it is also profoundly unconscious—a strange attribute, which at once fixes a gulf between it and our idea of a personal God. And accordingly, since Tao is the grand model for mankind, Chuang Tzŭ would have us strive to attain so far as may be to a like unconsciousness. But absolute and unbroken unconsciousness during this life being an impossibility, he advocates, not universal suicide, which would plainly violate the order of nature, but a state of mental abstraction which shall involve at least a total absence of self-consciousness. In order to explain his thought more clearly, he gives a number of vivid illustrations from life, such as the parable of Prince Hui's cook, who devoted himself to Tao and worked with his mind and not with his eye. He shows that the highest pitch of manual dexterity is attained only by those whose art has become their second nature, who have grown so familiar with their work that all their movements seem to come instinctively and of themselves, who, in other words, have reached the stage at which they are really "unconscious" of any effort. This application of Tao in the humble sphere of the handicraftsman serves to point the way towards the higher regions of abstract contemplation, where it will find its fullest scope. The same idea is carried into the domain of ethics. As we have seen, Chuang Tzŭ would have men neither moral nor immoral, but simply non-moral. And to this end every taint of self-consciousness must be purged away, the mind must be freed from its own criteria, and all one's trust must be placed in natural intuition. Any attempt to impose fixed standards of morality on the peoples of the earth is to be condemned, because it leaves no room for that spontaneous and unforced accord with nature which is the very salt of human action. Thus, were it feasible, Chuang Tzŭ would transport mankind back into the golden age which existed before the distinction between right and wrong arose. When the artificial barrier between contraries was set up, the world had already, in his eyes, lost its primitive goodness. For the mere fact of being able to call one's conduct good implies a lapse into the uncertain sea of relativity, and consequent deviation from the heavenly pattern. Herein lies the explanation of the paradox, on which he is constantly harping, that wisdom, charity, duty to one's neighbour and so on, are opposed to Tao.

It is small wonder that China has hesitated to adopt a system which logically leads to such extreme conclusions. Nevertheless, we must not too hastily write Chuang Tzŭ off as an unpractical dreamer. Remote though his speculations seem from the world of reality, they rest on a substratum of truth. In order to set forth his views with more startling effect, he certainly laid undue stress on the mystical side of Lao Tzŭ's philosophy, to the exclusion of much that was better worth handling. That he himself, however, was not altogether blind to the untenability of an extreme position may be gathered from a remark which he casually lets fall: "While there should be no action, there should be also no inaction." This is a pregnant saying, which shows how Chuang Tzŭ may have modified his stubborn attitude to meet the necessities of actual life. What he means is that any hard-and-fast, predetermined line of conduct is to be avoided, abstinence from action just as much as action itself. . The great thing is that nothing be done of set purpose when it seems to violate the natural order of events. On the other hand, if a certain course of action presents itself as the most obvious and natural to adopt, it would not be in accordance with Tao to shrink from it. This is known as the doctrine of inaction, but it would be more correctly named the doctrine of spontaneity.

There is another noteworthy element in Chuang Tzŭ's system which does much to smooth away the difficulty of reconciling theory and practice. This is what he calls the doctrine of non-angularity and self-adaptation to externals. It is really a corollary to the grand principle of getting outside one's personality—a process which extends the mental horizon and creates sympathy with the minds of others. Some such wholesome corrective was necessary to prevent the Taoist code from drifting into mere quixotry. Here again Lao Tzŭ may have supplied the seed which was to ripen in the pages of his disciple. "What the world reverences cannot be treated with disrespect," is the dictum of the older sage. But Chuang Tzŭ went beyond this negative precept. He saw well enough that unless a man is prepared to run his head against a stone wall, he must, in the modern cant phrase, adjust himself to his environment. Without abating a jot of his inmost convictions, he must "swim with the tide, so as not to offend others." Outwardly he may adapt himself, if inwardly he keeps up to his own standard. There must be no raging and tearing propaganda, but infinite patience and tact. Gentle moral suasion and personal example are the only methods that

Chuang Tzŭ will countenance; and even with these he urges caution: "If you are always offending others by your superiority, you will probably come to grief." Above all, he abhors the clumsy stupidity which would go on forcing its stock remedies down the people's throat irrespective of place or season. Thus even Confucius is blamed for trying to revive the dead ashes of the past and "make the customs of Chou succeed in Lu." This, he says, is like "pushing a boat on land, great trouble and no result, except certain injury to oneself." There must be no blind and rigid adherence to custom and tradition, no unreasoning worship of antiquity. "Dress up a monkey in the robes of Chou Kung,[5] and it will not be happy until they are torn to shreds. And the difference between past and present, " he adds bitterly, "is much the same as the difference between Chou Kung and a monkey." The rebuke conveyed in these remarks is not wholly unmerited. Chuang Tzŭ, while hardly yielding to Confucius himself in his ardent admiration of the olden time, never fell into the mistake of supposing that the world can stand still, though he feared it might sometimes go backward. He believed that to be the wisest statecraft, which could take account of changed conditions and suit its measures to the age. Plainly the inactivity he preached, hard though it be to fathom and harder still to compass, was something very different from stagnation. It was a lesson China needed; well for her in these latter days if she had taken it more to heart!

The comparative neglect of Chuang Tzŭ among the *literati* of the Middle Kingdom is no doubt chiefly due to his cavalier treatment of Confucius, of which we have just had a sample. Most of the writers who mention him speak of his hostile attitude towards the head of the orthodox school. As a matter of fact, this hostility has been a little exaggerated. For one thing, Chuang Tzŭ's attitude is by no means consistent; the tone adopted towards Confucius passes through every variety of shade. In the first seven chapters, which form the nucleus of Chuang Tzŭ's work, he is assigned a very prominent position, acting for the most part as the mouth-piece of the author's own views, which he is made to expound with an air of authority. In only one passage is he treated with disrespect, though in another it is implied that he was a prophet unsuited to his age. In chapter vi we may even discern a rough attempt at reconciling the two extremes of mystic Taoism and matter-of-fact Confucianism. It seems that all may not aspire to the more intimate communion with Tao, though Tao is the environment of all. For Confucius here resigns himself to the will of Heaven, which has ordained that he, like the bulk of mankind, shall travel within the ordinary "rule of life," with its limited outlook, its prejudices, forms, and ceremonies; but he frankly recognises the superior blessedness of the favoured few who can transcend it. In some of the later chapters (the genuineness of which is not always unimpeachable) the Master is more severely handled. Especially does he appear to disadvantage, as might naturally be expected, in his alleged interviews with Lao Tzŭ.[4] But in other places again he is represented as an earnest inquirer after truth, or even cited as an acknowledged authority. He quotes words which now stand in the *Tao Tê Ching*, and generally behaves more like a disciple of Lao Tzŭ than as the head of a rival system. In chapter xxii, by a strange piece of inadvertence, he is actually made to disparage the Confucianists with their scholastic quibbles. But it is in the last of the genuine chapters, entitled *Lieh Tzŭ*, that the acme of inconsistency is reached. Here Confucius is attacked as "a man of outward show and specious words. He mistakes the branch for the root." If entrusted with the welfare of the State, "it will only be by mistake that he will succeed." Yet this tirade is immediately followed by a characteristic harangue in the Taoist vein, delivered by no other than the much-maligned sage himself. It is hard, indeed, to imagine the central figure of the *Analects* speaking in this strain:—"There is nothing more fatal than intentional virtue, when the mind looks outwards. For by thus looking outwards, the power of introspection is destroyed. . . . What is it to aim at virtue? Why, a man who aims at virtue practises what he approves and condemns what he does not practise." Misrepresentation is carried to such lengths that sayings are put into his mouth which are the exact opposite of what he really uttered. And it is unlikely that Chuang Tzŭ had much scruple in thus harnessing the great Teacher to his own doctrines. He was doubtless fully alive to the advantage of borrowing and, as it were, absorbing the unparalleled prestige of so great a man; besides which, the sheer audacity of the scheme must have attracted him; and he carried it out with what the Confucianists are justified in regarding as the utmost effrontery. Yet it would be too much to say that this curious form of homage was wholly insincere. There are signs that Chuang Tzŭ was impressed, almost in spite of himself, by the pure personal character of the man whose whole view of life he distrusted, but whose message was so deeply printed in the hearts of his countrymen. He could not escape the common influence; the very frequency with which he brings Confucius upon the stage, whether as prophet or target for abuse, tells of a certain involuntary fascination.

The state of doubt in which we are left with regard to our author's real estimate of Confucius may serve to call attention to the peculiar ironical quality of his mind, which pleasantly tempers his dogmatism and, indeed, often saves him from a sharp descent into the ridiculous. It would almost seem as if, true to the Taoist precept, he were endeavouring to break through the restraining bonds of his individual self, and to contemplate his own judgments from the outside. Needless to say, there is a fount of deep, almost fierce, earnestness in the man as well. But he never loses a certain delicacy of touch which lends peculiar aptness to the sobriquet of "butterfly," bestowed on him in allusion to his famous dream. To these qualities must be added, in order to complete a faint sketch of this unique figure in Chinese literature, a recurrent strain of pervasive melancholy, a mournful brooding over "the doubtful doom of humankind." Take, for instance, these few lines picturing the mental faculties in their inevitable decline: "Then, as under autumn and winter's blight, comes gradual decay; a passing away, like the flow of water, never to return. Finally, the block, when all is choked up like an old drain,—the failing mind which shall not see light again." Just as the form of Chuang Tzŭ's work hovers on the borderland of poetry and prose, so the content is poetic rather than strictly philosophic, by reason of the lightness and grace with which he skims over subjects bristling with difficulty. Lucidity and precision of thought are sometimes sacrificed to imagination and beauty of style. He seldom attempts passages of sustained reasoning, but prefers to rely on flashes of literary inspiration. He is said to have shone in his verbal conflicts with Hui Tzŭ, but the specimens of his dialectic that have been preserved are, perhaps, more subtle than convincing. The episode of the minnows under the bridge only proves that in arguing with a sophist he could himself descend to sophistry naked and unabashed.

A noteworthy feature of Chuang Tzŭ's method is the wealth of illustration which he lavishes upon his favourite topics. In a hundred various ways he contrives to point the moral which is never far from his thoughts. Realising as fully as Herbert Spencer after him, the necessity of constant iteration in order to force alien conceptions on unwilling minds, he returns again and again to the cardinal points of his system, and skilfully arrays his arguments in an endless stream of episode and anecdote. These anecdotes are usually thrown into the form of dialogue—not the compact and closely-reasoned dialogue of Plato, but detached conversations between real or imaginary persons, sometimes easy in tone, sometimes declamatory, and here and there rising to fine heights of rhetoric. It may be objected to this method that it hinders the proper development of thought by destroying its continuity, and is therefore more suited to a merely popular work than to that of a really original thinker; on the other side it can only be urged that it lends dramatic colouring and relieves the tedium inseparable from a long philosophical treatise. The objection, on the whole, has much force, and yet it is equally true that the alternative method would have robbed Chuang Tzŭ's work of more than half its charm; its immortality is after all due less to the matter, much of which to modern notions is somewhat crude, than to the exquisite form. And certainly, as a means of fixing a principle in the mind, a single anecdote told by Chuang Tzŭ is worth reams of dry disquisition.

Though the difficulty of his text and the abstruseness of his theme have been a bar to very wide-spread popularity, Chuang Tzŭ has never lost favour with the select band of scholars. From time to time, when Taoism happened to be in fashion, he also enjoyed considerable vogue at Court. His book, like the *Tao Tê Ching*, formed the subject of lectures and examinations, and several Emperors are said to have studied and written upon it. In 713 A.D., it was specially decreed that those members of the public service should be singled out for promotion who were able to understand Chuang Tzŭ. That he was always considered a hard nut to crack is sufficiently shown by the flood of commentaries and other works devoted to his elucidation. Nevertheless, we are told as usual of a marvellous boy—one of the infant prodigies in whom Chinese annals are so rich—who at twelve years of age understood the meaning of both Lao Tzŭ and Chuang Tzŭ. The philosopher's works, in Kuo Hsiang's standard edition, were printed for the first time in the year 1005 A.D., and the reigning Emperor presented each of his Ministers with a copy.

Until we come to Lin Hsi-chung at the beginning of the present dynasty, native criticism cannot be said to have thrown any very dazzling light on our author. An early writer, who may possibly have seen him in the flesh, complains that "he hides himself in the clouds and has no knowledge of men." Another pronounces him "reckless, one who submitted to no law." From a third we learn that "in his desire to free himself from the trammels of objective existences, he lost himself in the quicksands of metaphysics." Sometimes he is damned with the faintest of praise: "In his teachings propriety plays no part, neither are they founded on eternal principles; nevertheless, they wear the semblance of wisdom and have their good points." On the other hand, rabid Confucianists insisted that "his book was expressly intended to cast a slur on their Master, in order to make people accept his own heterodox teaching; and, consequently, nothing would satisfy them but that his writings should be burnt and his disciples cut off. As to the rights and wrongs of his system, they were not even worth discussing."

From kindred poetic souls he has obtained more generous recognition. The great Po Chü-i, of the Tang dynasty, with whom he appears to have been a special favourite, was inspired by the perusal of his works to write three short poems, one of which contains the following stanzas[5]:

PEACEFUL OLD AGE

Chuang Tzŭ said: "Tao gives me this toil in manhood, this repose in old age, this rest in death."

Swiftly and soon the golden sun goes down,
The blue sky wells afar into the night;
Tao is the changeful world's environment,
Happy are they that in its laws delight.

Tao gives me toil—youth's passion to achieve,
And leisure in life's autumn and decay:
I follow Tao,—the seasons are my friends
Opposing it, misfortune comes my way.

****

Within my breast no sorrows can abide,
I feel the great world's spirit through me thrill

And as a cloud I drift before the wind,
Or with the random swallow take my will.
As underneath the mulberry tree I dream,
The water-clock drips on, and dawn appears:
A new day shines o'er wrinkles and white hair,
The symbols of the fulness of my years.

****

If I depart, I cast no look behind;
If still alive, I still am free from care.
Since life and death in cycles come and go,
Of little moment are the days to spare.
Thus strong in faith I wait and long to be
One with the pulsings of Eternity.

The Brahmanistic influence which these lines betray is faithfully reflected from Chuang Tzŭ. There are critics who would trace the same influence further back still, and regard the speculations of Lao Tzŭ himself as borrowed directly from India. But in the absence of any trustworthy evidence of communication between the two countries at that early date, the final verdict on this theory cannot yet be pronounced. With Chuang Tzŭ the case is somewhat different. The intervening period had seen the rise of Gautama and the spreading of a new and powerful religion which embodied in itself all the more essential parts of the Brahmanistic creed. By Chuang Tzŭ's time Buddhism had probably penetrated far and wide throughout Asia. It was not officially introduced into China until much later, but it seems only reasonable to suppose that driblets must have filtered through here and there. Certainly we find in the Chinese philosopher such striking points of similarity to Brahmanism as can hardly be explained as mere coincidences of thought. He believes, for instance, that every human being has a soul, which is an emanation from the great impersonal Soul of the universe. In contradistinction to the mind, which is only the scene or background of our ever-changing sensations and emotions, and dies with the body, the soul is in its nature immortal, and after passing through a series of different states in conditioned being, finally reunites with the divine essence whence it sprang. How to hasten the attainment of this goal of supreme bliss—that is the question which lies at the root of Chuang Tzŭ's philosophy. And his answer points to the abstract contemplation of Tao as the only means of destroying attachment to existence for its own sake, and thus loosening the soul from its bodily fetters. So far he resembles the Buddhist. But when he comes to touch on the contemplative life, we find him diverging from the recognised Buddhist ideal in one or two notable particulars. To him the highest form of virtue does not mean the mortification of animal instincts. Rather would he like these to have free and natural scope. Nor does it consist in living the life of a hermit. For "the perfect man can transcend the limits of the human and yet not withdraw from the world." "Those," he says, "who would benefit mankind from deep forests or lofty mountains are simply unequal to the strain upon their higher natures." Again, his hatred of outward show leads him to condemn anything approaching ritualism or asceticism, which he perceives truly enough to be symptoms of decay in the moral fibre. The only form of fasting he will recommend is the "fasting of the heart."

But divested thus of every shred of materialistic grossness, and converted into a purely spiritual creed, Taoism soon became altogether too shadowy and impalpable to stand alone against its formidable rival. It had to await the infusion of much-needed Buddhistic elements before it could re-assert itself as a national religion. This decline it was Chuang Tzŭ's fate to hasten rather than to arrest. His capital error lay in neglecting to develop those grand and simple moral truths with which Lao Tzŭ had leavened his abstruser speculations. The virtues of humility, gentleness and forgiveness of injury, which the earlier Taoist gospel held in such high esteem, are by him either passed over in silence or subordinated to the all-engrossing mystic purpose. Thus it was that the glowing promise of a singularly exalted moral code died away in later hands to the dust and ashes of a spurious metaphysic. No doubt, as a thorough-going exponent of his own principles, Chuang Tzŭ cared but little for outward and visible results. He was in no sense a propagandist; the kingdom of the mind was his real province. Yet the fact remains that the intellectual elevation and refinement of his system placed it beyond the grasp of all except a few; unlike Confucius, he made little or no provision for the struggling mass of mankind which could not be expected to rise to the higher planes of abstract thought.

This, however, is a criticism which leaves Chuang Tzŭ's literary position unaffected; and it is literature, after all, which claims the immortal part of his name and fame. For he of all the ancients wielded the most perfect mastery over Chinese prose style, and was the first to show to what heights of eloquence and beauty his native language could attain. And in these respects, great as the achievements are of which later Chinese literature can boast, he has never been surpassed. Indeed, his master-hand sounded chords that have vibrated since to no other touch. Finally, what effect may his writings be expected to produce on the modern Western mind? It is certain that to many, even through the necessarily imperfect medium of a translation, he already makes a powerful appeal; and it may at least be safely predicted that a far greater number of readers will be attracted by his originality and grace than repelled by the rather fantastic vagaries of his mysticism.

I. The Doctrine Of Relativity

In the northern ocean there is a fish, called the Leviathan, many thousand *li*[6] in size. This Leviathan changes into a bird, called the Rukh, whose back is many thousand *li* in breadth. With a mighty effort it rises, and its wings obscure the sky like clouds. At the equinox, this bird prepares to start for the southern ocean, the Celestial Lake. And in the *Record of Marvels* we read that when the rukh flies southwards, the water is smitten for a space of three thousand *li* around, while the bird itself mounts upon a typhoon to a height of ninety thousand *li*, for a flight of six months' duration. Just so are the motes in a sunbeam blown aloft by God. For whether the blue of the sky is its real colour, or only the result of distance without end, the effect to the bird looking down would be just the same as to the motes. . . . A cicada laughed, and said to a young dove, "Now, when I fly with all my might, 'tis as much as I can do to get from tree to tree. And sometimes I do not reach, but fall to the ground midway. What, then, can be the use of going up ninety thousand *li* in order to start for the south?" . . . Those two little creatures,—what should they know? Small knowledge has not the compass of great knowledge any more than a short year has the length of a long year. How can we tell that this is so? The mushroom of a morning knows not the alternation of day and night. The chrysalis knows not the alternation of spring and autumn. Theirs are short years. But in the State of Ch'u there is a tortoise whose spring and autumn are each of five hundred years' duration. And in former days there was a large tree which had a spring and autumn each of eight thousand years' duration. Yet P'êng Tsu[7] is still, alas! an object of envy to all.

****

There is nothing under the canopy of heaven greater than the tip of an autumn spikelet. A vast mountain is a small thing. Neither is there any age greater than that of a child cut off in infancy. P'êng Tsu himself died young. The universe and I came into being together; and I, and everything therein, are One.

****

It was the time of autumn floods. Every stream poured into the river, which swelled in its turbid course. The banks receded so far from each other that it was impossible to tell a cow from a horse.

Then the Spirit of the River laughed for joy that all the beauty of the earth was gathered to himself. Down with the stream he journeyed east until he reached the ocean. There, looking eastwards and seeing no limit to its waves, his countenance changed. And as he gazed over the expanse, he sighed and said to the Spirit of the Ocean, "A vulgar proverb says that he who has heard but part of the truth thinks no one equal to himself. And such a one am I.

"When formerly I heard people detracting from the learning of Confucius or underrating the heroism of Poh I, I did not believe. But now that I have looked upon your inexhaustibility—alas for me had I not reached your abode, I should have been for ever a laughing-stock to those of comprehensive enlightenment!"

To which the Spirit of the Ocean replied: "You cannot speak of ocean to a well-frog,—the creature of a narrower sphere. You cannot speak of ice to a summer insect,—the creature of a season. You cannot speak of Tao to a pedagogue: his scope is too restricted. But now that you have emerged from your narrow sphere and have seen the great ocean, you know your own insignificance, and I can speak to you of great principles. . .

"The Four Seas—are they not to the universe but like puddles in a marsh? The Middle Kingdom—is it not to the surrounding ocean like a tare-seed in a granary? Of all the myriad created things, man is but one. And of all those who inhabit the land, live on the fruit of the earth, and move about in cart and boat, an individual man is but one. Is not he, as compared with all creation, but as the tip of a hair upon a horse's skin?

"Dimensions are limitless; time is endless. Conditions are not invariable; terms are not final. Thus, the wise man looks into space, and does not regard the small as too little, nor the great as too much; for he knows that there is no limit to dimension. He looks back into the past, and does not grieve over what is far off, nor rejoice over what is near; for he knows that time is without end. He investigates fulness and decay, and does not rejoice if he succeeds, nor lament if he fails; for he knows that conditions are not invariable. He who clearly apprehends the scheme of existence does not rejoice over life, nor repine at death; for he knows that terms are not final.

"What man knows is not to be compared with what he does not know. The span of his existence is not to be compared with the span of his non-existence. With the small, to strive to exhaust the great necessarily lands him in confusion, and he does not attain his object. How then should one be able to say that the tip of a hair is the *ne plus ultra* of smallness, or that the universe is the *ne plus ultra* of greatness?"

****

Those who would have right without its correlative, wrong; or good government without its correlative, misrule,—they do not apprehend the great principles of the universe nor the conditions to which all creation is subject. One might as well talk of the existence of heaven without that of earth, or of the negative principle without the positive, which is clearly absurd.

****

If you adopt, as absolute, a standard of evenness which is so only relatively, your results will not be absolutely even. If you adopt, as absolute, a criterion of right which is so only relatively, your results will not be absolutely right. Those who trust to their senses become slaves to objective existences. Those alone who are guided by their intuitions find the true standard. So far are the senses less reliable than the intuitions. Yet fools trust to their senses to know what is good for mankind, with alas! but external results.

II. The Identity Of Contraries

Tzŭ Ch'i of Nan-kuo sat leaning on a table. Looking up to heaven, he sighed and became absent, as though soul and body had parted. Yen Chê'ng Tzŭ Yu, who was standing by him, exclaimed "What are you thinking about that your body should become thus like dry wood, your mind like dead ashes? Surely the man now leaning on the table is not he who was here just now."

"My friend," replied Tzŭ Ch'i, "your question is apposite. To-day I have buried myself. . . . Do you understand? . . . Ah! perhaps you only know the music of Man, and not that of Earth. Or even if you have heard the music of Earth, you have not heard the music of Heaven."

"Pray explain," said Tzŭ Yu.

"The breath of the universe," continued Tzŭ Ch'i, "is called wind. At times, it is inactive. But when active, every aperture resounds to the blast. Have you never listened to its growing roar? Caves and dells of hill and forest, hollows in huge trees of many a span in girth,—these are like nostrils, like mouths, like ears, like beam-sockets, like goblets, like mortars, like ditches, like bogs. And the wind goes rushing through them, sniffing, snoring, singing, soughing, puffing, purling, whistling, whirring, now shrilly treble, now deeply bass, now soft, now loud; until, with a lull, silence reigns supreme. Have you never witnessed among the trees such a disturbance as this?"

"Well, then," inquired Tzŭ Yu, "since the music of Earth consists of nothing more than holes, and the music of Man of pipes and flutes, of what consists the music of Heaven?"

"The effect of the wind upon these various apertures," replied Tzŭ Ch'i, "is not uniform. But what is it that gives to each the individuality, to all the potentiality, of sound? . . . Joy and anger, sorrow and happiness, caution and remorse, come upon us by turns, with ever-changing mood. They come like music from hollowness, like mushrooms from damp. Daily and nightly they alternate within us, but we cannot tell whence they spring. Can we then hope in a moment to lay our finger upon their very cause?

"But for these emotions, *I* should not be. But for *me*, they would have no scope. So far we can go; but we do not know what it is that brings them into play. 'Twould seem to be a *soul;* but the clue to its existence is wanting. That such a power operates is credible enough, though we cannot see its form. It has functions without form.

"Take the human body with all its manifold divisions. Which part of it does a man love best? Does he not cherish all equally, or has he a preference? Do not all equally serve him? And do these servitors then govern themselves, or are they subdivided into rulers and subjects? Surely there is some soul which sways them all.

"But whether or not we ascertain what are the functions of this soul, it matters but little to the soul itself. For, coming into existence with this mortal coil of mine, with the exhaustion of this mortal coil its mandate will also be exhausted. To be harassed by the wear and tear of life, and to pass rapidly through it without possibility of arresting one's course,—is not this pitiful indeed? To labour without ceasing, and then, without living to enjoy the fruit, worn out, to depart, suddenly, one knows not whither,—is not that a just cause for grief?

"What advantage is there in what men call not dying? The body decomposes, and the mind goes with it. This is our real cause for sorrow. Can the world be so dull as not to see this? Or is it I alone who am dull, and others not so? . . . There is nothing which is not objective: there is nothing which is not subjective. But it is impossible to start from the objective. Only from subjective knowledge is it possible to proceed to objective knowledge. Hence it has been said, 'The objective emanates from the subjective; the subjective is consequent upon the objective. This is the Alternation Theory.' Nevertheless, when one is born, the other dies. When one is possible, the other is impossible. When one is affirmative, the other is negative. Which being the case, the true sage rejects all distinctions of this and that. He takes his refuge in God, and places himself in subjective relation with all things.

"And inasmuch as the subjective is also objective, and the objective also subjective, and as the contraries under each are indistinguishably blended, does it not become impossible for us to say whether subjective and objective really exist at all?

"When subjective and objective are both without their correlates, that is the very axis of Tao. And when that axis passes through the centre at which all Infinities converge, positive and negative alike blend into an infinite One. . . Therefore it is that, viewed from the standpoint of Tao, a beam and a pillar are identical. So are ugliness and beauty, greatness, wickedness, perverseness, and strangeness. Separation is the same as construction: construction is the same as destruction. Nothing is subject either to construction or to destruction, for these conditions are brought together into One.

"Only the truly intelligent understand this principle of the identity of all things. They do not view things as apprehended by themselves, subjectively; but transfer themselves into the position of the things viewed. And viewing them thus they are able to comprehend them, nay, to master them; and he who can master them is near.[8] So it is that to place oneself in subjective relation with externals, without consciousness of their objectivity,—this is Tao. But to wear out one 's intellect in an obstinate adherence to the individuality of things, not recognising the fact that all things are One,—this is called *Three in the Morning*."

"What is *Three in the Morning?*" asked Tzŭ Yu.

"A keeper of monkeys," replied Tzŭ Chi, "said with regard to their rations of chestnuts, that each monkey was to have three in the morning and four at night. But at this the monkeys were very angry, so the keeper said they might have four in the morning and three at night, with which arrangement they were all well pleased. The actual number of the chestnuts remained the same, but there was an adaptation to the likes and dislikes of those concerned. Such is the principle of putting oneself into subjective relation with externals.

"Wherefore the true sage, while regarding contraries as identical, adapts himself to the laws of Heaven. This is called following two courses at once.

"The knowledge of the men of old had a limit. It extended back to a period when matter did not exist. That was the extreme point to which their knowledge reached. The second period was that of matter, but of matter unconditioned. The third epoch saw matter conditioned, but contraries were still unknown. When these appeared, Tao began to decline. And with the decline of Tao, individual bias arose."

III. Illusions

How do I know that love of life is not a delusion after all? How do I know but that he who dreads to die is as a child who has lost the way and cannot find his home?

The lady Li Chi was the daughter of Ai Fêng. When the Duke of Chin first got her, she wept until the bosom of her dress was drenched with tears. But when she came to the royal residence, and lived with the Duke, and ate rich food, she repented of having wept. How then do I know but that the dead repent of having previously clung to life?

Those who dream of the banquet wake to lamentation and sorrow. Those who dream of lamentation and sorrow wake to join the hunt. While they dream, they do not know that they dream. Some will even interpret the very dream they are dreaming; and only when they awake do they know it was a dream. By and by comes the Great Awakening, and then we find out that this life is really a great dream. Fools think they are awake now, and flatter themselves they know if they are really princes or peasants. Confucius and you are both dreams; and I who say you are dreams,—I am but a dream myself. This is a paradox. To-morrow a sage may arise to explain it; but that tomorrow will not be until ten thousand generations have gone by.

Granting that you and I argue. If you beat me, and not I you, are you necessarily right and I wrong? Or if I beat you and not you me, am I necessarily right and you wrong? Or are we both partly right and partly wrong? Or are we both wholly right or wholly wrong? You and I cannot know this, and consequently the world will be in ignorance of the truth.

Who shall I employ as arbiter between us? If I employ some one who takes your view, he will side with you. How can such a one arbitrate between us? If I employ some one who takes my view, he will side with me. How can such a one arbitrate between us? And if

I employ some one who either differs from or agrees with both of us, he will be equally unable to decide between us. Since then you, and I, and man, cannot decide, must we not depend upon Another? Such dependence is as though it were not dependence. We are embraced in the obliterating unity of God.

****

Once upon a time, I, Chuang dreamt I was a butterfly, fluttering hither and thither, to all intents and purposes a butterfly. I was conscious only of following my fancies as a butterfly, and was unconscious of my individuality as a man. Suddenly I awaked, and there I lay, myself again. Now I do not know whether I was then a man dreaming I was a butterfly, or whether I am now a butterfly dreaming I am a man. Between a man and a butterfly there is necessarily a barrier. The transition is called metempsychosis.

IV. The Mysterious Immanence Of Tao

The Penumbra said to the Umbra, "At one moment you move: at another you are at rest. At one moment you sit down: at another you get up. Why this instability of purpose?"

"I depend," replied the Umbra, "upon something which causes me to do as I do; and that something depends in turn upon something else which causes it to do as it does. My dependence is like that of a snake's scales or of a cicada's wings. How can I tell why I do one thing, or why I do not do another?"

****

Prince Hui's cook was cutting up a bullock. Every blow of his hand, every heave of his shoulders, every tread of his foot, every thrust of his knee, every *whshh* of rent flesh, every *chhk* of the chopper, was in perfect harmony,—rhythmical like the dance of the Mulberry Grove, simultaneous like the chords of the Ching Shou.

"Well done!" cried the Prince; "yours is skill indeed."

"Sire," replied the cook, "I have always devoted myself to Tao. It is better than skill. When I first began to cut up bullocks, I saw before me simply *whole* bullocks. After three years' practice, I saw no more whole animals. And now I work with my mind and not with my eye. When my senses bid me stop, but my mind urges me on, I fall back upon eternal principles. I follow such openings or cavities as there may be, according to the natural constitution of the animal. I do not attempt to cut through joints: still less through large bones.

"A good cook changes his chopper once a year,—because he cuts. An ordinary cook, once a month,—because he hacks. But I have had this chopper nineteen years, and although I have cut up many thousand bullocks, its edge is as if fresh from the whetstone. For at the joints there are always interstices, and the edge of a chopper being without thickness, it remains only to insert that which is without thickness into such an interstice.[9] By these means the interstice will be enlarged, and the blade will find plenty of room. It is thus that I have kept my chopper for nineteen years as though fresh from the whetstone.

"Nevertheless, when I come upon a hard part where the blade meets with a difficulty, I am all caution. I fix my eye on it. I stay my hand, and gently apply my blade, until with a *hwah* the part yields like earth crumbling to the ground. Then I take out my chopper, and stand up, and look around, and pause, until with an air of triumph I wipe my chopper and put it carefully away."

"Bravo!" cried the Prince. "From the words of this cook I have learnt how to take care of my life."

****

In the State of Chêng there was a wonderful magician named Chi Han. He knew all about birth and death, gain and loss, misfortune and happiness, long life and short life—predicting events to a day with supernatural accuracy. The people of Chêng used to flee at his approach; but Lieh Tzŭ went to see him, and became so infatuated that on his return he said to Hu Tzŭ,[10] "I used to look upon your Tao as perfect. Now I know something more perfect still."

"So far," replied Hu Tzŭ, "I have only taught you the ornamentals, not the essentials, of Tao; and yet you think you know all about it. Without cocks in your poultry-yard, what sort of eggs do the hens lay?[11] If you go about trying to force Tao down people's throats, you will be simply exposing yourself. Bring your friend with you, and let me show myself to him."

So next day Lieh Tzŭ went with Chi Han to see Hu Tzŭ, and when they came out Chi Han said: "Alas! your teacher is doomed. He cannot live. I hardly give him ten days. I am astonished at him. He is but wet ashes."

Lieh Tzŭ went in and wept bitterly, and told Hu Tzŭ; but the latter said: "I showed myself to him just now as the earth shows us its outward form, motionless and still, while production is all the time going on. I merely prevented him from seeing my pent-up energy within. Bring him again."

Next day the interview took place as before; but as they were leaving Chi Han said to Lieh Tzŭ: "It is lucky for your teacher that he met me. He is better. He will recover. I saw he had recuperative power."

Lieh Tzŭ went in and told Hu Tzŭ; whereupon the latter replied: "I showed myself to him just now as heaven shows itself in all its dispassionate grandeur, letting a little energy run out of my heels. He was thus able to detect that I had some. Bring him here again."

Next day a third interview took place, and as they were leaving, Chi Han said to Lieh Tzŭ: "Your teacher is never one day like another; I can tell nothing from his physiognomy. Get him to be regular, and I will then examine him again."

This being repeated to Hu Tzŭ as before, the latter said: "I showed myself to him just now in a state of harmonious equilibrium. Where the whale disports itself,—is the abyss. Where water is at rest,—is the abyss. Where water is in motion,—is the abyss. The abyss has nine names. These are three of them."[12]

Next day the two went once more to see Hu Tzŭ; but Chi Han was unable to stand still, and in his confusion turned and fled.

"Pursue him!" cried Hu Tzŭ; whereupon Lieh Tzŭ ran after him, but could not overtake him; so he returned and told Hu Tzŭ that the fugitive had disappeared.

"I showed myself to him just now," said Hu Tzŭ, "as Tao appeared before time was. I was to him as a great blank, existing of itself. He knew not who I was. His face fell. He became confused. And so he fled."

Upon this Lieh Tzŭ stood convinced that he had not yet acquired any real knowledge, and at once set to work in earnest, passing three years without leaving the house. He helped his wife to cook the family dinner, and fed his pigs just like human beings. He discarded the artificial and reverted to the natural. He became merely a shape. Amidst confusion he was unconfounded. And so he continued to the end.

****

Books are what the world values as representing Tao. But books are only words, and the valuable part of words is the thought therein contained. That thought has a certain bias which cannot be conveyed in words, yet the world values words as being the essence of books. But though the world values them, they are not of value; as that sense in which the world values them is not the sense in which they are valuable. . . .

Duke Huan was one day reading in his hall, when a wheelwright who was working below flung down his hammer and chisel, and mounting the steps said: "What words may your Highness be studying?"

"I am studying the words of the Sages," replied the Duke.

"Are the Sages alive?" asked the wheelwright.

"No," answered the Duke; "they are dead."

"Then the words your Highness is studying," rejoined the wheelwright, "are only the dregs of the ancients."

"What do you mean, sirrah!" cried the Duke, "by interfering with what I read? Explain yourself, or you shall die."

"Let me take an illustration," said the wheelwright, "from my own trade. In making a wheel, if you work too slowly, you can't make it firm; if you work too fast, the spokes won't fit in. You must go neither too slowly nor too fast. There must be co-ordination of mind and hand. Words cannot explain what it is, but there is some mysterious art herein. I cannot teach it to my son; nor can he learn it from me. Consequently, though seventy years of age, I am still making wheels in my old age. If the ancients, together with what they could not impart, are dead and gone, then what your Highness is studying must be the dregs."

****

A drunken man who falls out of a cart, though he may suffer, does not die. His bones are the same as other people's; but he meets his accident in a different way. His spirit is in a condition of security. He is not conscious of riding in the cart; neither is he conscious of falling out of it. Ideas of life, death, fear, etc., cannot penetrate his breast; and so he does not suffer from contact with objective existences. And if such security is to be got from wine, how much more is it to be got from God? It is in God that the Sage seeks his refuge, and so he is free from harm.

****

Lieh Yü K'ou instructed Po Hun Wu Jên in archery. Drawing the bow to its full, he placed a cup of water on his elbow and began to let fly. Hardly was one arrow out of sight ere another was on the string, the archer standing all the time like a statue.

"But this is shooting under ordinary conditions," cried Po Hun Wu Jen; "it is not shooting under extraordinary conditions. Now I will ascend a high mountain with you, and stand on the edge of a precipice a thousand feet in height, and see how you can shoot then."

Thereupon Wu Jên went with Lieh Tzŭ up a high mountain, and stood on the edge of a precipice a thousand feet in height, approaching it backwards until one-fifth of his feet overhung the chasm, when he beckoned to Lieh Tzŭ to come on. But the latter had fallen prostrate on the ground, with the sweat pouring down to his heels.

"The perfect man," said Wu Jen, "soars up to the blue sky, or dives down to the yellow springs,[13] or flies to some extreme point of the compass, without change of countenance. But you are terrified, and your eyes are dazed. Your internal economy is

defective.
”

****

A disciple said to Lu Chü: "Master, I have attained to your Tao. I can do without fire in winter. I can make ice in summer."

"You merely avail yourself of latent heat and latent cold," replied Lu Chü. "That is not what I call Tao. I will demonstrate to you what my Tao is."

Thereupon he tuned two lutes, and placed one in the hall and the other in the adjoining room. And when he struck the *kung* note on one, the *kung* note on the other sounded; when he struck the *chio* note on one, the *chio* note on the other sounded. This because they were both tuned to the same pitch.

But if he changed the interval of one string, so that it no longer kept its place in the octave, and then struck it, the result was that all the twenty-five strings jangled together. There was sound as before, but the influence of the key-note was gone.

V. The Hidden Spring

Tao has its laws and its evidences. It is devoid both of action and of form. It may be transmitted, but cannot be received. It may be obtained, but cannot be seen. Before heaven and earth were, Tao was. It has existed without change from all time. Spiritual beings drew their spirituality therefrom, while the universe became what we can see it now. To Tao, the zenith is not high, nor the nadir low; no point in time is long ago, nor by lapse of ages has it grown old.

Hsi Wei[14] obtained Tao, and so set the universe in order. Fu Hsi[15] obtained it, and was able to establish eternal principles. The Great Bear obtained it, and has never erred from its course. The sun and moon obtained it, and have never ceased to revolve.

****

Chuang Tzŭ said: "O my exemplar! Thou who destroyest all things, and dost not account it cruelty; thou who benefitest all time, and dost not account it charity; thou who art older than antiquity and dost not account it age; thou who supportest the universe, shaping the many forms therein, and dost not account it skill; this is the happiness of God!"

****

Life follows upon death. Death is the beginning of life. Who knows when the end is reached? The life of man results from convergence of the vital fluid. Its convergence is life; its dispersion, death. If, then, life and death are but consecutive states, what need have I to complain?

Therefore all things are One. What we love is animation. What we hate is corruption. But corruption in its turn becomes animation, and animation once more becomes corruption.

****

The universe is very beautiful, yet it says nothing. The four seasons abide by a fixed law, yet they are not heard. All creation is based upon absolute principles, yet nothing speaks.

And the true Sage, taking his stand upon the beauty of the universe, pierces the principles of created things. Hence the saying that the perfect man does nothing, the true Sage performs nothing, beyond gazing at the universe.

For man's intellect, however keen, face to face with the countless evolutions of things, their death and birth, their squareness and roundness,—can never reach the root. There creation is, and there it has ever been.

The six cardinal points, reaching into infinity, are ever included in Tao. An autumn spikelet, in all its minuteness, must carry Tao within itself. There is nothing on earth which does not rise and fall, but it never perishes altogether. The *Yin* and the *Yang*.[16] and the four seasons, keep to their proper order. Apparently destroyed, yet really existing; the material gone, the immaterial left,—such is the law of creation, which passeth all understanding. This is called the root, whence a glimpse may be obtained of God.

****

A man's knowledge is limited; but it is upon what he does not know that he depends to extend his knowledge to the apprehension of God.

Knowledge of the great One, of the great Negative, of the great Nomenclature, of the great Uniformity, of the great Space, of the great Truth, of the great Law,—this is perfection. The great One is omnipresent. The great Negative is omnipotent. The great Nomenclature is all-inclusive. The great Uniformity is all-assimilative. The great Space is all-receptive. The great Truth is all-exacting. The great Law is all-binding.

The ultimate end is God. He is manifested in the laws of nature. He is the hidden spring. At the beginning, he was. This, however, is inexplicable. It is unknowable. But from the unknowable we reach the known.

Investigation must not be limited, nor must it be unlimited. In this undefinedness there is an actuality. Time does not change it. It cannot suffer diminution. May we not, then, call it our great Guide?

Why not bring our doubting hearts to investigation thereof? And then, using certainty to dispel doubt, revert to a state without doubt, in which doubt is doubly dead?

****

"Chi Chên," said Shao Chih, "taught *Chance;* Chieh Tzŭ taught *Predestination.* In the speculations of these two schools, on which side did right lie?"

"The cock crows," replied T'ai Kung Tiao, "and the dog barks. So much we know. But the wisest of us could not say why one crows and the other barks, nor guess why they crow or bark at all.

"Let me explain. The infinitely small is inappreciable; the infinitely great is immeasurable. Chance and Predestination must refer to the conditioned. Consequently, both are wrong.

"Predestination involves a real existence. Chance implies an absolute absence of any principle. To have a name and the embodiment thereof,—this is to have a material existence. To have no name and no embodiment,—of this one can speak and think; but the more one speaks the farther off one gets.

"The unborn creature cannot be kept from life. The dead cannot be tracked. From birth to death is but a span; yet the secret cannot be known. Chance and Predestination are but *à priori* solutions.

"When I seek for a beginning, I find only time infinite. When I look forward to an end, I see only time infinite. Infinity of time past and to come implies no beginning and is in accordance with the laws of material existences. Predestination and Chance give us a beginning, but one which is compatible only with the existence of matter.

"Tao cannot be existent. If it were existent, it could not be non-existent. The very name of Tao is only adopted for convenience' sake. Predestination and Chance are limited to material existences. How can they bear upon the infinite?

"Were language adequate, it would take but a day fully to set forth Tao. Not being adequate, it takes that time to explain material existences. Tao is something beyond material existences. It cannot be conveyed either by words or by silence. In that state which is neither speech nor silence, its transcendental nature may be apprehended."

****

All things spring from germs. Under many diverse forms these things are ever being reproduced. Round and round, like a wheel, no part of which is more the starting-point than any other. This is called heavenly equilibrium. And he who holds the scales is God.

****

Life has its distinctions; but in death we are all made equal. That death should have an origin, but that life should have no origin,—can this be so? What determines its presence in one place, its absence in another? Heaven has its fixed order. Earth has yielded up its secrets to man. But where to seek whence am I?

Not knowing the hereafter, how can we deny the operation of Destiny? Not knowing what preceded birth, how can we assert the operation of Destiny? When things turn out as they ought, who shall say that the agency is not supernatural? When things turn out otherwise, who shall say that it is?

VI. Non-Interference With Nature

Horses have hoofs to carry them over frost and snow; hair, to protect them from wind and cold. They eat grass and drink water, and fling up their heels over the champaign. Such is the real nature of horses. Palatial dwellings are of no use to them.

One day Po Lo appeared, saying: "I understand the management of horses."

So he branded them, and clipped them, and pared their hoofs, and put halters on them, tying them up by the head and shackling them by the feet, and disposing them in stables, with the result that two or three in every ten died. Then he kept them hungry and thirsty, trotting them and galloping them, and grooming, and trimming, with the misery of the tasselled bridle before and the fear of the knotted whip behind, until more than half of them were dead.

The potter says: "I can do what I will with clay. If I want it round, I use compasses; if rectangular, a square."

The carpenter says: "I can do what I will with wood. If I want it curved, I use an arc; if straight, a line."

But on what grounds can we think that the natures of clay and wood desire this application of compasses and square, of arc and line? Nevertheless, every age extols Po Lo for his skill in managing horses, and potters and carpenters for their skill with clay and wood. Those who govern the empire make the same mistake.

Now I regard government of the empire from quite a different point of view.

The people have certain natural instincts:—to weave and clothe themselves, to till and feed. themselves. These are common to all humanity, and all are agreed thereon. Such instincts are called "Heaven-sent."

And so in the days when natural instincts prevailed, men moved quietly and gazed steadily. At that time, there were no roads over mountains, nor boats, nor bridges over water. All things were produced, each for its own proper sphere. Birds and beasts multiplied; trees and shrubs grew up. The former might be led by the hand; you could climb up and peep into the raven's nest. For then man dwelt with birds and beasts, and all creation was one. There were no distinctions of good and bad men. Being all equally without knowledge, their virtue could not go astray. Being all equally without evil desires they were in a state of natural integrity, the perfection of human existence.

But when Sages appeared, tripping up people over charity and fettering them with duty to their neighbour, doubt found its way into the world. And then, with their gushing over music and fussing over ceremony, the empire became divided against itself.

VII. Passive Virtue

Yen Hui[17] went to take leave of Confucius.

"Whither are you bound?" asked the master.

"I am going to the State of Wei," was the reply.

"And what do you propose to do there?" continued Confucius.

"I hear," answered Yen Hui, "that the Prince of Wei is of mature age, but of an unmanageable disposition. He behaves as if the State were of no account, and will not see his own faults. Consequently, the people perish; and their corpses lie about like so much undergrowth in a marsh. They are at extremities. And I have heard you, sir, say that if a State is well governed it may be neglected; but that if it is badly governed, then we should visit it. The science of medicine embraces many various diseases. I would test my knowledge in this sense, that perchance I may do some good to that State."

"Alas!" cried Confucius, "you will only succeed in bringing evil upon yourself. For Tao must not be distributed. If it is, it will lose its unity. If it loses its unity, it will be uncertain; and so cause mental disturbance,—from which there is no escape.

"The Sages of old first got Tao for themselves, and then got it for others. Before you possess this yourself, what leisure have you to attend to the doings of wicked men? Besides, do you know what Virtue results in, and where Wisdom ends? Virtue results in a desire for fame; wisdom ends in contentions. In the struggle for fame men crush one another, while their wisdom but provokes rivalry. Both are baleful instruments, and may not be incautiously used. . . . But of course you have a scheme. Tell it to me."

"Gravity of demeanour," replied Yen Hui, "and dispassionateness; energy and singleness of purpose,—will this do?"

"Alas!" said Confucius, "that will not do. If you make a show of being perfect and obtrude yourself, the Prince's mood will be doubtful. Ordinarily, he is not opposed, and so he has come to take actual pleasure in trampling upon the feelings of others. And if he has thus failed in the practice of routine virtues, do you expect that he will take readily to higher ones? You may insist, but without result. Outwardly you will be right, but inwardly wrong. How then will you make him mend his ways? . . Your firmness will secure you from harm; but that is all. You will not influence him to such an extent that he shall seem to follow the dictates of his own heart."

"Then," said Yen Hui, "I am without resource, and venture to ask for a method."

Confucius said: "*Fast!* . . . Let me explain. You have here a method, but it is difficult to practise. Those which are easy are not from God."

"Well," replied Yen Hui, "my family is poor, and for many months we have tasted neither wine nor flesh. Is not that fasting?"

"The fasting of religious observance it is," answered Confucius, "but not the fasting of the heart."

"And may I ask," said Yen Hui, "in what consists the fasting of the heart?"

"Cultivate unity," replied Confucius. "You hear not with the ears, but with the mind; not with the mind, but with your soul. But let hearing stop with the ears. Let the working of the mind stop with itself. Then the soul will be a negative existence, passively responsive to externals. In such a negative existence, only Tao can abide. And that negative state is the fasting of the heart."

"Then," said Yen Hui, "the reason I could not get the use of this method is my own individuality. If I could get the use of it, my individuality would have gone. Is this what you mean by the negative state?"

"Exactly so," replied the Master. "Let me tell you. If you can enter this man's domain without offending his *amour propre*, cheerful if he hears you, passive if he does not; without science, without drugs, simply living there in a state of complete indifference,—you will be near success. . . . Look at that window. Through it an empty room becomes bright with scenery; but the landscape stops outside. . . . In this sense, you may use your ears and eyes to communicate within, but shut out all wisdom from the mind. . . . This is the method for regenerating all creation."

****

Duke Ai of the Lu State said to Confucius: "In the Wei State there is a leper named Ai T'ai T'o. The men who live with him like him and make no effort to get rid of him. Of the women who have seen him, many have said to their parents, Rather than be another man's wife, I would be his concubine.

"He never preaches at people, but puts himself into sympathy with them, He wields no power by which he may protect men's bodies. He has at his disposal no appointments by which to gratify their hearts. He is loathsome to a degree. He sympathises, but does not instruct. His knowledge is limited to his own state. Yet males and females alike all congregate around him.

"So thinking that he must be different from ordinary men, I sent for him, and saw that he was indeed loathsome to a degree. Yet we had not been many months together ere my attention was fixed upon his conduct. A year had not elapsed ere I trusted him thoroughly; and as my State wanted a Prime Minister, I offered the post to him. He accepted it sullenly, as if he would much rather have declined. Perhaps he did not think me good enough for him! At any rate, he took it; but in a very short time he left me and went away. I grieved for him as for a lost friend, and as though there were none left with whom I could rejoice. What manner of man is this?"

"When I was on a mission to the Ch'u State," replied Confucius, "I saw a litter of young pigs sucking their dead mother. After a while they looked at her, and then they all left the body and went off. For their mother did not look at them any more, nor did she any more seem to be of their kind. What they loved was their mother; not the body which contained her, but that which made the body what it was. . . .

"Now Ai T'ai T'o says nothing, and is trusted. He does nothing, and is sought after. He causes a man to offer him the government of his own State, and the only fear is lest he should decline. Truly his talents are perfect, and his virtue without outward form!"

"What do you mean by his talents being perfect?" asked the Duke.

"Life and Death," replied Confucius, "existence and non-existence, success and nonsuccess, poverty and wealth, virtue and vice, good and evil report, hunger and thirst, warmth and cold,—these all revolve upon the changing wheel of Destiny. Day and night they follow one upon the other, and no man can say where each one begins. Therefore they cannot be allowed to disturb the harmony of the organism, nor enter into the soul's domain. Swim however with the tide, so as not to offend others. Do this day by day without break, and live in peace with mankind. Thus you will be ready for all contingencies, and may be said to have your talents perfect."

"And virtue without outward form; what is that?"

"In a water-level," said Confucius, "the water is in a most perfect state of repose. Let that be your model. The water remains quietly within, and does not overflow. It is from the cultivation of such harmony that virtue results. And if virtue takes no outward form, man will not be able to keep aloof from it."

****

"Tell me," said Lao Tzŭ, "in what consist charity and duty to one's neighbour?"

"They consist," answered Confucius, "in a capacity for rejoicing in all things; in universal love, without the element of self. These are the characteristics of charity and duty to one's neighbour."

"What stuff!" cried Lao "Does not universal love contradict itself? Is not your elimination of self a positive manifestation of self? Sir, if you would cause the empire not to lose its source of nourishment,—there is the universe, its regularity is unceasing; there are the sun and moon, their brightness is unceasing; there are the stars, their groupings never change; there are birds and beasts, they flock together without varying; there are trees and shrubs, they grow upwards without exception. Be like these; follow Tao; and you will be perfect. Why then these vain struggles after charity and duty to one's neighbour, as though beating a drum in search of a fugitive? Alas! sir, you have brought much confusion into the mind of man."

****

Suppose a boat is crossing a river, and another empty boat is about to collide with it. Even an irritable man would not lose his temper. But supposing there was some one in the second boat. Then the occupant of the first would shout to him to keep clear. And if the other did not hear the first time, nor even when called to three times, bad language would inevitably follow. In the first case there was no anger, in the second there was; because in the first case the boat was empty, and in the second it was occupied. And so it is with man. If he could only roam empty through life, who would be able to injure him?

VIII. Self-Adaptation To Externals

Yen Ho was about to become tutor to the eldest son of Prince Ling of the Wei State. Accordingly he observed to Chü Po Yü: "Here is a man whose disposition is naturally of a low order. To let him take his own unprincipled way is to endanger the State. Tot try to restrain him is to endanger one's personal safety. He has just wit enough to see faults in others, but not to see his own. I am consequently at a loss what to do."

"A good question, indeed," replied Chü Po Yü; "you must be careful, and begin by self- reformation. Outwardly you may adapt yourself, but inwardly you must keep up to your own standard. In this there are two points to be guarded against. You must not let the outward adaptation penetrate within, nor the inward standard manifest itself without. In the former case, you will fall, you will be obliterated, you will collapse, you will lie prostrate. In the latter case you will be a sound, a name, a bogie, an uncanny thing. If he would play the child, do you play the child too. If he cast aside all sense of decorum, do you do so too. As far as he goes, do you go also. Thus you will reach him without offending him.

"Don't you know the story of the praying-mantis? In its rage it stretched out its arms to prevent a chariot from passing, unaware that this was beyond its strength, so admirable was its energy! Be cautious. If you are always offending others by your superiority, you will probably come to grief.

"Do you not know that those who keep tigers do not venture to give them live animals as food, for fear of exciting their fury when killing the prey? Also, that whole animals are not given, for fear of exciting the tiger's fury when rending them? The periods of hunger and repletion are carefully watched in order to prevent such outbursts. The tiger is of a different species from man; but the latter too is manageable if properly treated, unmanageable if excited to fury.

"Those who are fond of horses surround them with various conveniences. Sometimes mosquitoes or flies trouble them; and then, unexpectedly to the animal, a groom will brush them off, the result being that the horse breaks his bridle, and hurts his head and chest. The intention is good, but there is a want of real care for the horse. Against this you must be on your guard."

****

For travelling by water there is nothing like a boat. For travelling by land there is nothing like a cart. This because a boat moves readily in water; but were you to try to push it on land you would never succeed in making it go. Now ancient and modern times may be likened unto water and land; Chou and Lu to the boat and the cart. To try to make the customs of Chou succeed in Lu, is like pushing a boat on land: great trouble and no result, except certain injury to oneself. . . .

Dress up a monkey in the robes of Chou Kung, and it will not be happy until they are torn to shreds. And the difference between past and present is much the same as the difference between Chou Kung and a monkey.

****

When Hsi Shih[18] was distressed in mind, she knitted her brows. An ugly woman of the village, seeing how beautiful she looked, went home, and having worked herself into a fit frame of mind, knitted her brows. The result was that the rich people of the place barred up their doors and would not come out, while the poor people took their wives and children and departed elsewhere. That woman saw the beauty of knitted brows, but she did not see wherein the beauty of knitted brows lay.

****

Kuan Chung being at the point of death, Duke Huan went to see him.

"You are venerable Sir," said the Duke, "really ill. You had better say to whom, in the event of your getting worse, I am to entrust the administration of the State."

"Whom does your Highness wish to choose?" inquired Kuan Chung.

"Will Pao Yü do?" asked the Duke.

"He will not," said Kuan Chung. "He is pure, incorruptible, and good. With those who are not like himself he will not associate. And if he has once heard of a man's wrong-doing, he never forgets it. If you employ him in the administration of the empire, he will get to loggerheads with his prince and to sixes and sevens with the people. It would not be long before he and your Highness fell out."

"Whom then can we have?" asked the Duke.

"There is no alternative," replied Kuan Chung; "it must be Hsi P'êng. He is a man who forgets the authority of those above him, and makes those below him forget his. Ashamed that he is not the peer of the Yellow Emperor, he grieves over those who are not the peers of himself.

"To share one's virtue with others is called true wisdom. To share one's wealth with others is reckoned meritorious. To exhibit superior merit is not the way to win men's hearts. To exhibit inferior merit is the way. There are things in the State he does not hear; there are things in the family he does not see. There is no alternative; it must be Hsi P'êng."

****

To glorify the past and to condemn the present has always been the way of the scholar. Yet if Hsi Wei Shih[19] and individuals of that class were caused to re-appear in the present day, which of them but would accommodate himself to the age?

IX. Immortality Of The Soul

When Lao Tzŭ died, Ch'in Shih went to mourn. He uttered three yells and departed.

A disciple asked him, saying: "Were you not our Master's friend?"

"I was," replied Ch'in Shih.

"And if so, do you consider that a sufficient expression of grief at his loss?" added the disciple.

"I do," said Ch'in Shih. "I had believed him to be the man of all men, but now I know that he was not. When I went in to mourn, I found old persons weeping as if for their children, young ones wailing as if for their mothers. And for him to have gained the attachment of those people in this way, he too must have uttered words which should not have been spoken, and dropped tears which should not have been shed, thus violating eternal principles, increasing the sum of human emotion, and forgetting the source from which his own life was received. The ancients called such emotions the trammels of mortality. The Master came, because it was his time to be born; he went, because it was his time to die. For those who accept the phenomenon of birth and death in this sense, lamentation and sorrow have no place. The ancients spoke of death as of God cutting down a man suspended in the air. The fuel is consumed, but the fire may be transmitted, and we know not that it comes to an end.

****

To have attained to the human form must be always a source of joy. And then, to undergo countless transitions, with only the infinite to look forward to,—what incomparable bliss is that! Therefore it is that the truly wise rejoice in that which can never be lost, but endures alway.

****

A son must go whithersoever his parents bid him. Nature is no other than a man's parents. If she bid me die quickly, and I demur, then I am an unfilial son. She can do me no wrong. Tao gives me this form, this toil in manhood, this repose in old age, this rest in death. And surely that which is such a kind arbiter of my life is the best arbiter of my death.

Suppose that the boiling metal in a smelting-pot were to bubble up and say: "Make of me an Excalibur"; I think the caster would reject that metal as uncanny. And if a sinner like myself were to say to God: "Make of me a man, make of me a man"; I think he too would reject me as uncanny. The universe is the smelting-pot, and God is the caster. I shall go whithersoever I am sent, to wake unconscious of the past, as a man wakes from a dreamless sleep.

****

Chuang Tzŭ one day saw an empty skull, bleached, but still preserving its shape. Striking it with his riding-whip, he said: "Wert thou once some ambitious citizen whose inordinate yearnings brought him to this pass?—some statesman who plunged his country into ruin and perished in the fray?—some wretch who left behind him a legacy of shame?—some beggar who died in the pangs of hunger and cold? Or didst thou reach this state by the natural course of old age?"

When he had finished speaking, he took the skull and, placing it under his head as a pillow, went to sleep. In the night he dreamt that the skull appeared to him and said: "You speak well, sir; but all you say has reference to the life of mortals, and to mortal troubles. In death there are none of these. Would you like to hear about death?"

Chuang Tzŭ having replied in the affirmative, the skull began: "In death there is no sovereign above, and no subject below. The workings of the four seasons are unknown. Our existences are bounded only by eternity. The happiness of a king among men cannot exceed that which we enjoy."

Chuang Tzŭ, however, was not convinced, and said:

"Were I to prevail upon God to allow your body to be born again, and your bones and flesh to be renewed, so that you could return to your parents, to your wife, and to the friends of your youth,—would you be willing?"

At this the skull opened its eyes wide and knitted its brows and said: "How should I cast aside happiness greater than that of a king, and mingle once again in the toils and troubles of mortality?"

X. The Sage, Or Perfect Man

The perfect man ignores self; the divine man ignores action; the true Sage ignores reputation.

****

The perfect man is a spiritual being. Were the ocean itself scorched up, he would not feel hot. Were the Milky Way frozen hard, he would not feel cold. Were the mountains to be riven with thunder, and the great deep to be thrown up by storm, he would not tremble.

****

How does the Sage seat himself by the sun and moon, and hold the universe in his grasp? He blends everything into one harmonious whole, rejecting the confusion of this and that. Rank and precedence, which the vulgar prize, the Sage stolidly ignores. The revolutions of ten thousand years leave his unity unscathed. The universe itself may pass away, but he will flourish still.

****

With the truly wise, wisdom is a curse, sincerity like glue, virtue only a means to acquire, and skill nothing more than a commercial capacity. For the truly wise make no plans, and therefore require no wisdom. They do not separate, and therefore require no glue. They want nothing, and therefore need no virtue. They sell nothing, and therefore are not in want of a commercial capacity. These four qualifications are bestowed upon them by God and serve as heavenly food to them. And those who thus feed upon the divine have little need for the human. They wear the forms of men, without human passions. Because they wear the forms of men, they associate with men. Because they have not human passions, positives and negatives find in them no place. Infinitesimal, indeed, is that which makes them man; infinitely great is that which makes them divine!

Hui Tzŭ said to Chuang Tzŭ: "Are there, then, men who have no passions?"

Chuang Tzŭ replied: "Certainly."

"But if a man has no passions," argued Hui Tzŭ, "what is it that makes him a man?"

"Tao," replied Chuang Tzŭ, "gives him his expression, and God gives him his form. How should he not be a man?"

"If, then, he is a man," said Hui Tzŭ, "how can he be without passions?"

"What you mean by passions," answered Chuang Tzŭ, "is not what I mean. By a man without passions I mean one who does not permit good and evil to disturb his internal economy, but rather falls in with whatever happens, as a matter of course, and does not add to the sum of his mortality."

****

He who knows what God is, and who knows what Man is, has attained. Knowing what God is, he knows that he himself proceeded therefrom. Knowing what Man is, he rests in the knowledge of the known, waiting for the knowledge of the unknown. Working out one's allotted span, and not perishing in mid career,—this is the fulness of knowledge.

Herein, however, there is a flaw. Knowledge is dependent upon fulfilment. And as this fulfilment is uncertain, how can it be known that my divine is not really human, my human really divine? We must have *pure men*, and then only can we have *pure knowledge*.

But what is a pure man?—The pure men of old acted without calculation, not seeking to secure results. They laid no plans. Therefore, failing, they had no cause for regret; succeeding, no cause for congratulation. And thus they could scale heights without fear; enter water without becoming wet; fire, without feeling hot. So far had their wisdom advanced towards Tao.

The pure men of old slept without dreams, and waked without anxiety. They ate without discrimination, breathing deep breaths.

For pure men draw breath from their uttermost depths; the vulgar only from their throats. Out of the crooked, words are retched up like vomit. If men's passions are deep, their divinity is shallow.

The pure men of old did not know what it was to love life nor to hate death. They did not rejoice in birth, nor strive to put off dissolution. Quickly come and quickly go;—no more. They did not forget whence it was they had sprung, neither did they seek to hasten their return thither. Cheerfully they played their allotted parts, waiting patiently for the end. This is what is called not to lead the heart astray from Tao, nor to let the human seek to supplement the divine. And this is what is meant by a pure man.

****

The pure men of old did their duty to their neighbours, but did not associate with them. They behaved as though wanting in themselves, but without flattering others. Naturally rectangular, they were not uncompromisingly hard. They manifested their independence without going to extremes. They appeared to smile as if pleased, when the expression was only a natural response. Their outward semblance derived its fascination from the store of goodness within. They seemed to be of the world around them, while proudly treading beyond its limits. They seemed to desire silence, while in truth they had dispensed with language. They saw in penal laws a trunk[20]; in social ceremonies, wings[21]; in wisdom, a useful accessory; in morality, a guide. For them penal laws meant a merciful administration; social ceremonies, a passport through the world; wisdom, an excuse for doing what they could not help; and morality, walking like others upon the path. And thus all men praised them for the worthy lives they led.

****

The repose of the Sage is not what the world calls repose. His repose is the result of his mental attitude. All creation could not disturb his equilibrium: hence his repose. When water is still, it is like a mirror, reflecting the beard and the eyebrows. It gives the accuracy of the water-level, and the philosopher makes it his model. And if water thus derives lucidity from stillness, how much more the faculties of the mind! The mind of the Sage, being in repose, becomes the mirror of the universe, the speculum of all creation.

****

The truly great man, although he does not injure others, does not credit himself with charity and mercy. He seeks not gain, but does not despise his followers who do. He struggles not for wealth, but does not take credit for letting it alone. He asks help from no man, but takes no credit for his self-reliance, neither does he despise those who seek preferment through friends. He acts differently from the vulgar crowd, but takes no credit for his exceptionality; nor, because others act with the majority, does he despise them as hypocrites. The ranks and emoluments of the world are to him no cause for joy; its punishments and shame no cause for disgrace. He knows that positive and negative cannot be distinguished, that great and small cannot be defined.

****

The true Sage ignores God. He ignores man. He ignores a beginning. He ignores matter. He moves in harmony with his generation and suffers not. He takes things as they come and is not overwhelmed. How are we to become like him?

****

The true Sage is a passive agent. If he succeeds, he simply feels that he was provided by no effort of his own with the energy necessary to success.

****

External punishments are inflicted by metal and wood. Internal punishments are inflicted by anxiety and remorse. Fools who incur external punishment are treated with metal or wood. Those who incur internal punishment are devoured by the conflict of emotions. It is only the pure and perfect man who can succeed in avoiding both.

XI. Random Gleanings

TAKE no heed of time, nor of right and wrong; but, passing into the realm of the Infinite, take your final rest therein.

****

Our life has a limit, but knowledge is without limit.

****

To serve one's prince without reference to the act, but only to the service, is the perfection of a subject's loyalty.

****

In trials of skill, at first all is friendliness; but at last it is all antagonism.

****

Tzŭ Ch'i of Nan-po was travelling on the Shang mountain when he saw a large tree which astonished him very much. A thousand chariot teams could have found shelter under its shade.

"What tree is this?" cried Tzŭ Ch'i. "Surely it must have unusually fine timber." Then, looking up, he saw that its branches were too crooked for rafters; while, as to the trunk, he saw that its irregular grain made it valueless for coffins. He tasted a leaf, but it took the skin off his lips; and its odour was so strong that it would make a man as it were drunk for three days together.

"Ah!" said Tzŭ Ch'i. "This tree is good for nothing, and that is how it has attained this size. A wise man might well follow its example."

****

A man does not seek to see himself in running water, but in still water. For only what is itself still can instil stillness into others.

****

Is Confucius a Sage, or is he not? How is it he has so many disciples? He aims at being a subtle dialectician, not knowing that such a reputation is regarded by real Sages as the fetters of a criminal.

****

He who delights in man is himself not a perfect man. His affection is not true charity. Depending upon opportunity, he has not true worth. He who is not conversant with both good and evil is not a superior man. He who disregards his reputation is not what a man should be. He who is not absolutely oblivious of his own existence can never be a ruler of men.

****

When the pond dries up, and the fishes are left upon dry ground, to moisten them with the breath, or to damp them with spittle, is not to be compared with leaving them, in the first instance, in their native rivers and lakes. And better than praising Yao[22] and blaming Chieh[23] would be leaving them both and attending to the development of Tao.

****

Fishes are born in water. Man is born in Tao. If fishes get ponds to live in, they thrive. If man gets Tao to live in, he may live his life in peace.

****

"May I ask," said Tzŭ Kung, "about divine men?"

"Divine men," replied Confucius, "are divine to man, but ordinary to God. Hence the saying that the meanest being in heaven would be the best on earth; and the best on earth, the meanest in heaven."

****

The goodness of a wise ruler covers the whole empire, yet he himself seems to know it not. It influences all creation, yet none is conscious thereof. It appears under countless forms, bringing joy to all things. It is based upon the baseless, and travels through the realms of Nowhere.

****

By inaction one can become the centre of thought, the focus of responsibility, the arbiter of wisdom. Full allowance must be made for others, while remaining unmoved oneself. There must be a thorough compliance with divine principles, without any manifestation thereof. All of which may be summed up in the one word passivity. For the perfect man employs his mind as a mirror. It grasps nothing: it refuses nothing. It receives, but does not keep. And thus he can triumph over matter, without injury to himself.

****

Every addition to or deviation from nature belongs not to the ultimate perfection of all. He who would attain to such perfection never loses sight of the natural conditions of his existence. With him the joined is not united, nor the separated apart, nor the long in excess, nor the short wanting. For just as a duck's legs, though short, cannot be lengthened without pain to the duck, and a crane's legs, though long, cannot be shortened without misery to the crane, so that which is long in man's moral nature cannot be cut off, nor that which is short be lengthened. All sorrow is thus avoided.

****

What I mean by perfection is not what is meant by charity and duty to one's neighbour. It is found in the cultivation of Tao. And those whom I regard as cultivators of Tao are not those who cultivate charity and duty to one's neighbour. They are those who yield to the natural conditions of things. What I call perfection of hearing is not hearing others, but oneself. What I call perfection of vision is not seeing others, but oneself. For a man who sees not himself, but others, takes not possession of himself, but of others, thus taking what others should take and not what he himself should take. Instead of being himself, he in fact becomes some one else.

****

Ts'ui Chü asked Lao saying: "If the empire is not to be governed, how are men's hearts to be kept in order?"

"Be careful," replied Lao "not to interfere with the natural goodness of the heart of man. Man's heart may be forced down or stirred up. In each case the issue is fatal."

****

The men of this world all rejoice in others being like themselves, and object to others not being like themselves.

****

If metal and stone were without Tao, they would not be capable of emitting sound. And just as they possess the property of sound, but will not emit sound unless struck, so surely is the same principle applicable to all creation.

****

In the Golden Age good men were not appreciated; ability was not conspicuous. Rulers were mere beacons, while the people were free as the wild deer. They were upright without being conscious of duty to their neighbours. They loved one another without being conscious of charity. They were true without being conscious of loyalty. They were honest without being conscious of good faith. They acted freely in all things without recognising obligations to any one. Thus their deeds left no trace; their affairs were not handed down to posterity.

****

A man who knows that he is a fool is not a great fool.

****

Appeal to arms is the lowest form of virtue. Rewards and punishments are the lowest form of education. Ceremonies and laws are the lowest form of government. Music and fine clothes are the lowest form of happiness. Weeping and mourning are the lowest form of grief. These five should follow the movements of the mind. The ancients indeed cultivated the study of accidentals, but they did not allow it to precede that of essentials.

****

It is easy to be respectfully filial, but difficult to be affectionately filial. But even that is easier than to become unconscious of one's natural obligations, which is in turn easier than to cause others to be unconscious of the operations thereof. Similarly, this is easier than to become altogether unconscious of the world, which again is easier than to cause the world to be unconscious of one's influence upon it.

****

Charity and duty to one's neighbour are as caravanserais established by wise rulers of old; you may stop there one night, but not for long, or you will incur reproach.

****

Both small and great things must equally possess form. The mind cannot picture to itself a thing without form, nor conceive a form of unlimited dimensions. The greatness of anything may be a topic of discussion, or the smallness of anything may be mentally realised. But that which can be neither a topic of discussion nor realised mentally, can be neither great nor small.

****

The life of man passes by like a galloping horse, changing at every turn, at every hour. What should he do, or what should he not do, other than let his decomposition go on?

****

As to what the world does and the way in which people are happy now, I know not whether such happiness be real happiness or not. The happiness of ordinary persons seems to me to consist in slavishly following the majority, as if they could not help it. Yet they all say they are happy. But I cannot say that this is happiness or that it is not happiness. Is there, then, after all, such a thing as happiness?

I make true pleasure to consist in *inaction*, which the world regards as great pain. Thus it has been said, Perfect happiness is the absence of happiness."

****

A man who plays for counters will play well. If he stakes his girdle,[24] he will be nervous; if yellow gold, he will lose his wits. His skill is the same in each case, but he is distracted by the value of his stake. And every one who attaches importance to the external, becomes internally without resource.

****

The Grand Augur, in his ceremonial robes, approached the shambles and thus addressed the pigs: "How can you object to die? I shall fatten you for three months. I shall discipline myself for ten days and fast for three. I shall strew fine grass, and place you bodily upon a carved sacrificial dish. Does not this satisfy you?"

Then, speaking from the pigs' point of view, he continued: "It is better, perhaps, after all, to live on bran and escape the shambles. . . ."

"But then," added he, speaking from his own point of view, "to enjoy honour when alive one would readily die on a war-shield or in the headsman's basket."

So he rejected the pigs' point of view and adopted his own point of view. In what sense, then, was he different from the pigs?

****

When Yang Tzŭ went to the Sung State, he passed a night at an inn. The innkeeper had: two concubines—one beautiful, the other ugly. The latter he loved; the former he hated. Yang Tzŭ asked how this was; whereupon one of the inn servants said: "The beautiful one is so conscious of her beauty that one does not think her beautiful. The ugly one is so conscious of her ugliness that one does not think her ugly."

"Note this, my disciples!" cried Yang

"Be virtuous, but without being consciously so; and wherever you go, you will be beloved."

****

Shun asked Ch'êng, saying: "Can one get Tao so as to have it for one's own?"

"Your very body," replied Ch'êng, "is not your own. How should Tao be?"

"If my body," said Shun, "is not my own, pray whose is it?"

"It is the delegated image of God," replied Ch'êng. "Your life is not your own. It is the delegated harmony of God. Your individuality is not your own. It is the delegated adaptability of God. Your posterity is not your own. It is the delegated exuviæ of God. You move, but know not how. You are at rest, but know not why. You taste, but know not the cause. These are the operation of God's laws. How then should you get Tao so as to have it for your own?"

****

Man passes through this sublunary life as a sunbeam passes a crack—here one moment, gone the next.

****

Mountain forests and loamy fields swell my heart with joy. But ere the joy be passed, sorrow is upon me again. Joy and sorrow come and go, and over them I have no control.

Alas! the life of man is but as a stoppage at an inn. He knows that which comes within the range of his experience. Otherwise, he knows not. He knows that he can do what he can do, and that he cannot do what he cannot do. But there is always that which he does not know and that which he cannot do; and to struggle that it shall not be so—is not this a cause for grief?

The best language is that which is not spoken, the best form of action is that which is without deeds.

Spread out your knowledge, and it will be found to be shallow.

****

As to Yao and Shun, what claim have they to praise? Their fine distinctions simply amounted to knocking a hole in a wall in order to stop it up with brambles; to combing each individual hair; to counting the grains for a rice pudding! How in the name of goodness did they profit their generation?

****

Let knowledge stop at the unknowable. That is perfection.

****

There is no weapon so deadly as man's will. Excalibur is second to it. There is no bandit so powerful as Nature. In the whole universe there is no escape from it. Yet it is not Nature which does the injury. It is man's own heart.

****

Birth is not a beginning; death is not an end.

****

Discard the stimuli of purpose. Free the mind from disturbances. Get rid of entanglements to virtue. Pierce the obstructions to Tao.

****

A one-legged man discards ornament, his exterior not being open to commendation. Condemned criminals will go up to great heights without fear, for they no longer regard life and death from their former point of view. And those who pay no attention to their moral clothing and condition become oblivious of their own personality; and by thus becoming oblivious of their personality, they proceed to be the people of God.

Wherefore, if men revere them, they rejoice not. If men insult them, they are not angered. But only those who have passed into the eternal harmony of God are capable of this.

If your anger is external, not internal, it will be anger proceeding from not-anger. If your actions are external, not internal, they will be actions proceeding from inaction. If you would attain peace, level down your emotional nature. If you desire spirituality, cultivate adaptation of the intelligence. If you would have your actions in accordance with what is right, allow yourself to fall in with the dictates of necessity. For necessity is the Tao of the Sage.

****

If schemers have nothing to give them anxiety, they are not happy. If dialecticians have not their premisses and conclusions, they are not happy. If critics have none on whom to vent their spleen, they are not happy. Such men are the slaves of objective existences.

****

A dog is not considered a good dog because he is a good barker. A man is not considered a good man because he is a good talker.

****

The rulers of old set off all success to the credit of their people, attributing all failure to themselves.

****

When Chü Po Yü reached his sixtieth year, he changed his opinions. What he had previously regarded as right, he now came to regard as wrong. But who shall say whether the right of to-day may not be as wrong as the wrong of the previous fifty-nine years?

****

Shao Chih asked T'ai Kung Tiao, saying: "What is meant by society?"

"Society," replied T'ai Kung Tiao, "is an agreement of a certain number of families and individuals to abide by certain customs. Discordant elements unite to form a harmonious whole. Take away this unity, and each has a separate individuality.

"Point at any one of the many parts of a horse, and that is not a horse, although there is the horse before you. It is the combination of all which makes the horse.

"Similarly, a mountain is high because of its individual particles. A river is large because of its individual drops. And he is a just man who regards all parts from the point of view of the whole. Thus, in regard to the views of others, he holds his own opinion, but not obstinately. In regard to his own views, while conscious of their truth, he does not despise the opinions of others."

****

Wood rubbed with wood produces fire. Metal exposed to fire will liquefy. If the Positive and Negative principles operate inharmoniously, heaven and earth are greatly disturbed. Thunder crashes, and with rain comes lightning, scorching up the tall locust-trees. . . . So in the struggle between peace and unrest, the friction between good and evil, much fire is evolved which consumes the inner harmony of man. But the mind is unable to resist fire. It is destroyed, and with it Tao comes to an end.

****

Get rid of small wisdom, and great wisdom will shine upon you. Put away goodness and you will be naturally good. A child does not learn to speak because taught by professors of the art, but because it lives among people who can themselves speak.

****

Man has for himself a spacious domain. His mind may roam to heaven. If there is no room in the house, the wife and her mother-in-law run against one another. If the mind cannot roam to heaven, the faculties will be in a state of antagonism.

****

The *raison d'être* of a fish-trap is the fish. When the fish is caught, the trap may be ignored. The *raison d'être* of a rabbit-snare is the rabbit. When the rabbit is caught, the snare may be ignored. The *raison d'être* of language is an idea to be expressed. When the idea is expressed, the language may be ignored, But where shall I find a man to ignore language, with whom I may be able to converse?

****

Alas! man's knowledge reaches to the hair on a hair, but not to eternal peace.

****

The heart of man is more dangerous than mountains and rivers, more difficult to understand than Heaven itself. Heaven has its periods of spring, summer, autumn, winter, daytime and night. Man has an impenetrable exterior, and his motives are inscrutable. Thus some men appear to be retiring when they are really forward. Others have abilities, yet appear to be worthless. Others are compliant, yet gain their ends. Others take a firm stand, yet yield the point. Others go slow, yet advance quickly.

XII. Personal Anecdotes

Chuang Tzŭ was fishing in the P'u when the prince of Ch'u sent two high officials to ask him to take charge of the administration of the Ch'u State.

Chuang Tzŭ went on fishing and, without turning his head, said "I have heard that in Ch'u there is a sacred tortoise which has been dead now some three thousand years, and that the prince keeps this tortoise carefully enclosed in a chest on the altar of his ancestral temple. Now would this tortoise rather be dead and have its remains venerated, or be alive and wagging its tail in the mud?"

"It would rather be alive," replied the two officials, "and wagging its tail in the mud."

"Begone!" cried Chuang Tzŭ. "I too will wag my tail in the mud."

****

Hui Tzŭ was prime minister in the Liang State. Chuang Tzŭ went thither to visit him.

Some one remarked: "Chuang Tzŭ has come. He wants to be minister in your place," Thereupon Hui Tzŭ was afraid, and searched all over the State for three days and three nights to find him.

Then Chuang Tzŭ went to see Hui Tzŭ and said: "In the south there is a bird. It is a kind of Do you know it? It started from the south sea to fly to the north sea. Except on the *wu-t'ung* tree, it would not alight. It would eat nothing but the fruit of the bamboo, drink nothing but the purest spring water. An owl which had got the rotten carcass of a rat, looked up as the phoenix flew by, and screeched. Are you not screeching at me over your kingdom of Liang?"

****

Chuang Tzŭ and Hui Tzŭ had strolled on to the bridge over the Hao, when the former observed: "See how the minnows are darting about! That is the pleasure of fishes."

"You not being a fish yourself," said Hui Tzŭ, "how can you possibly know in what consists the pleasure of fishes?"

"And you not being I," retorted Chuang Tzŭ, "how can you know that I do not know?"

"If I, not being you, cannot know what you know," urged Hui Tzŭ, "it follows that you, not being a fish, cannot know in what consists the pleasure of fishes."

"Let us go back," said Chuang Tzŭ, "to your original question. You asked me how I knew in what consists the pleasure of fishes. Your very question shows that you knew I knew.[25] I knew it from my own feelings on this bridge."

****

When Chuang Tzŭ's wife died, Hui Tzŭ went to condole. He found the widower sitting on the ground, singing, with his legs spread out at a right angle, and beating time on a bowl.

"To live with your wife," exclaimed Hui Tzŭ, "and see your eldest son grow up to be a man, and then not to shed a tear over her corpse,—this would be bad enough. But to drum on a bowl, and sing; surely this is going too far."

"Not at all," replied Chuang Tzŭ. "When she died, I could not help being affected by her death. Soon, however, I remembered that she had already existed in a previous state before birth, without form, or even substance; that while in that unconditioned condition, substance was added to spirit; that this substance then assumed form; and that the next stage was birth. And now, by virtue of a further change, she is dead, passing from one phase to another like the sequence of spring, summer, autumn and winter. And while she is thus lying asleep in Eternity, for me to go about weeping and wailing would be to proclaim myself ignorant of these natural laws. Therefore I refrain."

****

When Chuang Tzŭ was about to die, his disciples expressed a wish to give him a splendid funeral. But Chuang Tzŭ said: "With Heaven and Earth for my coffin and shell; with the sun, moon, and stars, as my burial regalia; and with all creation to escort me to the grave,—are not my funeral paraphernalia ready to hand?"

"We fear," argued the disciples, "lest the carrion kite should eat the body of our Master;" to which Chuang Tzŭ replied: "Above ground I shall be food for kites; below I shall be food for mole-crickets and ants. Why rob one to feed the other?"